RANGER THE GALLOPER

"It is not who you are that hold you back. It's who you think you are not"

Suzana N.A.A. Amo-Mensah

AuthorHouse™ UK
1663 Liberty Drive
Bloomington, IN 47403 USA
www.authorhouse.co.uk
UK TFN: 0800 0148641 (Toll Free inside the UK)
UK Local: 02036 956322 (+44 20 3695 6322 from outside the UK)

Any people depicted in stock imagery provided by Getty Images are models, and such images are being used for illustrative purposes only. Certain stock imagery © Getty Images.

This book is printed on acid-free paper.

ISBN: 979-8-8230-8163-4 (sc)
ISBN: 979-8-8230-8162-7 (e)

Print information available on the last page.

Published by AuthorHouse 03/21/2023

Because of the dynamic nature of the Internet, any web addresses or links contained in this book may have changed since publication and may no longer be valid. The views expressed in this work are solely those of the author and do not necessarily reflect the views of the publisher, and the publisher hereby disclaims any responsibility for them.

authorHOUSE®

RANGER THE GALLOPER

There lived a beautiful white horse called Fancy in a small farm town called Wakefield. She was loved and adored by her owners, Mr. and Mrs. Hamilton.

Fancy was such an amazing galloper. She loved to be adorned with a beautiful saddle and accessories when she had competitions. Mr. and Mrs. Hamilton were a very creative couple and always made sure Fancy had a new look during competitions. The villagers admired her and sang her praises, and other horses could only look on in admiration.

Horse owners also adorned their horses during competitions in beautiful, colorful accessories to the delight of the audience, but none matched that of Fancy. She always looked exquisite.

Because her owners went all out and beyond for her, Fancy also made sure she trained well for all competitions. She actually won all the horse race competitions in the town.

3

Wakefield was a small but happy village. On weekends, the villagers gathered in a popular Inn called The "Power Rangers Inn." The Inn had an open space outside, decorated with benches made out of tree trunks with straw umbrellas stuck in the middle, providing shade from the sunlight in the day.

At night, the space glows as the fairy string light is put on. It was always beautiful scenery at night.

On Saturday afternoons, most of the town fellas met at the Inn. The men brewed fresh millet beer, and the women grilled steaks. They always looked forward to weekends as there was so much to eat and drink. They played games, sang, and danced the night away.

The people living in Wakefield knew each other and helped each other. They were farmers, and most villagers owned horses because the horse race always brought tourists to their town, and they made money for themselves in their famous horse competitions as the villagers set up food and drink stands to sell to visitors.

The next big town close to Wakefield was miles away, so the people resorted to growing their food and livestock. They usually sell their produce at the market square or do batter trading.

Fancy is old now. She has been running for 25 years and no longer has the energy and strength. She wanted to continue the legacy. Winning most of the race had made her famous in Wakefield and the neighboring towns, and she so much loved the attention and comfort she got over the years from the Villagers and her owners.

Fancy had two sons, Ninja and Ranger. Ninja had a leg injury during training years ago, so he no longer participates in competitions. Ranger was the youngest, always shy, and did not like to mingle. Ranger was a white horse just like his mother but had a big black patch on his face, which he did not like. He felt ugly all the time, and that gave him a withdrawn attitude.

One evening in their stable, Fancy called her sons to have a conversation with them.

"My dear sons," Fancy said, "You both know how much I love you. I am growing old, and I cannot compete in the town's horse races anymore. We need to keep the legacy running in the family."

"Ranger, my darling," Fancy continued, "You have all it takes to compete on behalf of the family."

"I don't want to compete in any silly race!" Ranger angrily blurted out.

"Hold your tongue, young man, before I push my hoof down your throat. Why are you always this angry, son?"

"I am sorry, mother. I didn't mean to be disrespectful." "It's ok, son," Fancy replied.

"As I was saying, there is an upcoming race in two weeks. This race is huge, and the neighboring town folks will be in attendance. The prize is huge, and I think it will be amazing if we win. You know Mr. and Mrs. Hamilton have loved us. This cash prize could go a long way to help them change their leaking roof."

"My darling son, Ranger, you need to train and represent us," Fancy said.

"Can I at least think about it, mum?"

Fancy did not know Ranger had issues with the black patch on his face. He never really spoke about it.

In her opinion, it was a unique birthmark, and she loved it.

Meanwhile, Ranger was very anxious. He had so much going through his mind. What if the crowd booed at him? What if the crowd laughed at him? He began to panic.

Ranger had a sleepless night that day. He was restless all through the night, thinking of all the possible things that could go wrong. He felt afraid. A part of him did not want to disappoint his mother and the Hamiltons.

I have a plan, he thought to himself. I will run far away into the forest where no one can find me.

It was a Monday afternoon, and training had started. Ranger was on the field ready to train but had his plan in mind. During the training, he was to run from one end of the field to another in timed seconds. Ranger ran as fast as he could and disappeared. Mr. and Mrs. Hamilton looked on in shock.

"Heyyy! Ranger," they shouted after him. But Ranger was gone.

"What is wrong with Ranger, Fancy?" Mrs. Hamilton asked.

Fancy felt so ashamed. She could not utter a word. She bowed her head and walked away with a sad face.

As she walked, she wondered what was wrong with her son. There must be something wrong with Ranger. She thought to herself. I will go find him.

Fancy galloped as fast as she could into the forest calling Ranger.

"Ranger, Ranger…" Fancy called. "I know you can hear me, son."

Fancy began to sob uncontrollably. As she laid on the floor sobbing, she heard a sound and lifted her head. Ranger was standing by her with a very sad face. "I knew you were close. I love you, son. And I am sorry for pushing you so hard to run the race without considering what or how you felt."

You don't have to do it. I will train and run on behalf of the family.

"Mum, I'm sorry. I shouldn't have run off. I am anxious and afraid of being ridiculed.

Fancy took a step back, looking confused. She repeated his words, "Scared, anxious, and afraid of being ridiculed?" "What makes you anxious and afraid of being ridiculed, son?" she asked, concerned.

"Look at my face, mum," Ranger sobbed, "I have got this black patch on my face. I am Ugly, mum. Other horses look more beautiful than I do, and I am sure they will laugh at me and call me names –the white horse with a black patch face."

"Oh, Ranger," Fancy said. "I had no idea you were uncomfortable with your patch. I have always thought it was beautiful. You were born unique, son. If 10 white horses were kidnapped with you included, they would easily be found because you were in their midst. Your patch is part of who you are. I had no idea you hated it."

"No one will care about your patch if you put on a show. You need to prove everyone wrong by training hard to win the race. Fame and success go beyond appearance. Be confident, son. You are the son of the famous Fancy, and you were named after the first famous horse runner in our town.

How you look does not affect your ability to run. Don't focus on what people say about it. Focus on the win. When you win, people will want to be your friend without you asking them."

"I will make you and the Hamiltons proud."

"I am sorry," he continued to sob.

Ranger began to sob, "I'm really sorry, mum. You raised me to face my fears, and I failed. I am sorry," he continued to sob.

"Thank you, my son," Fancy responded. "Let's get going." "Give me a few minutes, mum, I will be with you shortly." "Promise, son?" Fancy asked. "I promise, mum."

And with that, Fancy walked away. Ranger sat down quietly. Tears run down his face. His mum's words kept ringing in his head. He was also thinking to himself. Mum ran after me to search for me. Mr. and Mrs. Hamilton are worried and sick about me, and my brother, Ninja, cannot run because he has a hoof injury. I owe it to myself and my family to showcase my skills and win the prize. Come to think of it..he thought my patched face is part of who I am. It will never go away. What am I doing, sulking about what I cannot change? Gosh! Ranger. What's wrong with you? How could you be this mean to yourself? He stood up, wiped his face, and ran back home.

He got to the training ground where Mr. and Mrs. Hamilton, Fancy, and Ninja stood. They all smiled at him and gave him a hug. "I am sorry, family. I am ready now." Everyone jubilated.

Mr. Hamilton tied Ranger's hoof, and training began. Ranger trained so hard every day for 6 weeks.

Mrs. Hamilton spent time sewing and embroidering the most beautiful horse Saddle and head accessory. Knowing the caliber of people attending this race, she wanted Ranger to stand out.

The week before the race was going to come off, the people of Wakefield did a lot of communal labor to clean up the town. They decorated the sports center and set up food tents. They used all the resources they had in the community and did an amazing job. Everyone felt so proud of themselves.

It was Saturday morning. And the day of the race has come. Guests from neighboring towns had arrived. The town was full. Soon, it was time for the horses to line up. The horses stood in their section looking so glamorous in their track, but of course, Ranger stood out. The horses that stood next to him stole glances at him in admiration. In a few seconds, the gunshot went off, and the race began.

Ranger ran like the speed of light while the audience cheered on.

"He was actually phenomenal," an onlooker was heard saying. Ranger got to the finish line in less than 60 seconds, beating his mum's record of 65 seconds in her first game.

Everyone jubilated. Fancy was so excited she was seen dancing, and other horses joined in to celebrate with her. It was beautiful, and Ranger felt really good about the feat.

The horses were all rewarded, and Ranger received the grand prize, which was a check of 10,000 pounds that went to her owners.

That night, there was a huge party at the Power Ranger's Inn. The people partied, danced, and shared a meal and their favorite millet beer. Many congratulated Ranger, including his competitors. Ranger became famous in Wakefield and neighboring towns. Everyone wanted to be his friend, and it felt good.

He never looked down on himself. He learned to love himself and won more races. A statue of Fancy and Ranger was mounted at the entrance of Wakefield. The town became a tourist attraction site.

Lesson: Never look down on yourself. Positive self-image gives you confidence which will catapult you to success. When voices in your head keep downplaying you, always use positive affirmations to lift yourself up.

Speak and Believe

Words of Affirmation

* I am enough.
  * I get better every single day.
    * I am an amazing person.
* Whatever I do, I do it to the best of my ability.
  * Today I am a leader.
    * I forgive myself for my mistakes.
      * My challenges help me grow.
      * I am perfect just the way I am.
* My mistakes help me learn and grow.
  * If at first I don't succeed, I try again.
    * I have courage and confidence.
      * I can control my own happiness.
* I have people who love and respect me.
    * I stand up for what I believe in.
      * I believe in my goals and dreams.
      * It's okay not to know everything.
      * Today I choose to think positively.
        * I can get through anything.
          * I never ever give up.
* There is no one better to be than myself.

QUOTES

"Remind yourself that you cannot fail at being yourself."

"No one can make you feel inferior without your consent." ~Eleanor Roosevelt

"A strong, positive self-image is the best possible preparation for success." ~Joyce Brothers

"You are what you believe yourself to be." ~Paulo Coelho

"Believe in yourself a little more."

If ever you find yourself doubting you can make it through a challenge, simply think back to everything you have overcome in the past." ~Karen Salmansohn

Write 5 amazing qualities/strengths about yourself.

* ....

* ....

* ....

* ....

* ....

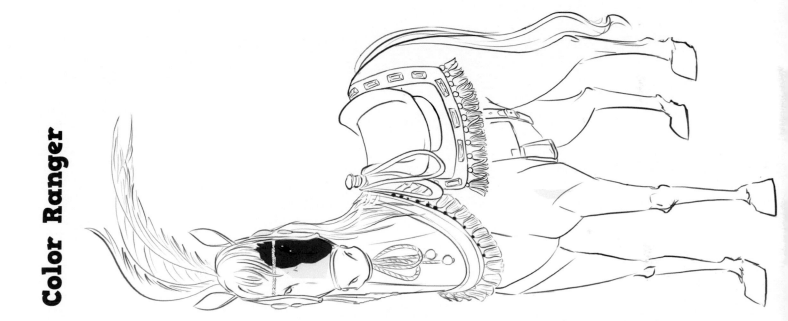

Color Ranger

Printed in the United States
by Baker & Taylor Publisher Services